Adrian MITCHELL'S GREATEST HITS

ERIC
BLOO
DAXE

BLOODAXE BOOKS

ISBN: 1 85224 164 0

First published 1991 by
Bloodaxe Books Ltd,
P.O. Box 1SN,
Newcastle upon Tyne NE99 1SN.

Bloodaxe Books Ltd acknowledges
the financial assistance of Northern Arts.

EDUCATIONAL HEALTH WARNING

None of the work in this or any of Adrian Mitchell's books
is to be used in connection with any examination whatsoever.
(But he is happy if they're read aloud in schools by people
who like them enough to read them aloud.)

Cover reproduction by V & H Reprographics, Newcastle upon Tyne.

Printed in Great Britain by
Bell & Bain Limited, Glasgow, Scotland.

ADRIAN MITCHELL'S
GREATEST HITS

John Colet

LIBRARY

Books available by Adrian Mitchell

POETRY

For Beauty Douglas: Collected Poems 1953-79 (Allison & Busby, 1982)
Love Songs of World War Three (Allison & Busby/W.H. Allen, 1989)
Greatest Hits: His 40 Golden Greats (Bloodaxe Books, 1991)

PLAYS

Calderón: The Mayor of Zalamea & two other plays (Absolute Classics)
Lope de Vega: Fuente Ovejuna and Lost in a Mirror (Absolute Classics)

POETRY FOR CHILDREN

Nothingmas Day (Allison & Busby, 1984)
Strawberry Drums, (Simon & Schuster, 1989)
All My Own Stuff, with Georgie Adams (Simon & Schuster, 1991)

CHILDREN'S STORIES

Our Mammoth
Our Mammoth Goes to School
Our Mammoth in the Snow

The Baron Rides Out
The Baron on the Island of Cheese
The Baron All at Sea

   (all Walker Books)

This book is for Celia, Alistair, Danny, Briony Sasha, Beattie, Natasha and Charlotte, with much love.

Acknowledgements

All these poems have been performed in many places, and my first thanks are to the organisers and audiences who encouraged me. All the poems have appeared in various magazines and anthologies and some of them in TV and radio programmes and even in newspapers.

They have also appeared in the following books: *Poems, Out Loud, Ride the Nightmare, The Apeman Cometh* (all published by Jonathan Cape), *For Beauty Douglas, On the Beach at Cambridge, Nothingmas Day* and *Love Songs of World War Three* (all Allison & Busby), and *Strawberry Drums* and *All My Own Stuff* (both Simon & Schuster).

The Top 40

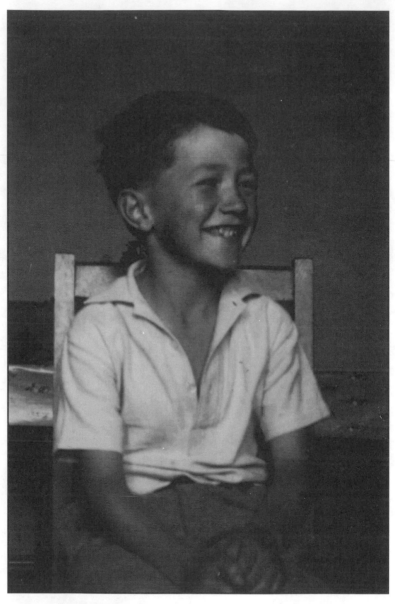

Adrian Mitchell listening to his first Fats Waller record, 1941.

A-one and a-two and you all know what to do!

The night was cool and the moon was yellow
And the leaves came tumbling down –
DE-DAH! DE-DAH! DE-DAH!

That's the intro to Lloyd Price's *Stagger Lee* and the wildest beginning to any record I know and so I borrow it as the lead in to the *Top Ten Questions* I'm asked at poetry shows. Nowadays I often declare a question time after the half-time Tizer break. I leave a pile of filing cards on the poem table and ask for written questions. This way I have a few seconds to think before answering and the shyer members of the throng get a look in. (This trick of written questions was stolen from Mayakovsky, who sometimes used to pop his own written questions himself into the hat and answer them very wittily.) Omitting such classic queries as 'Why are your trousers so long?', I've used some of these questions in this introduction. For this is the Introduction so will you please put your hands together for…

The Top Ten Questions

1. *Why Greatest Hits? Why Top Forty? Isn't that pretty vulgar? How can you expect to be taken seriously as a poet?*

A newspaper in County Durham once advertised a reading like this: 'ADRIAN MITCHELL AND HIS POULTRY'. It was a great audience, apart from the rooster. Why Greatest Hits? These are the forty poems which people ask for most often after my performances. They can't always afford the four books in which nearly all my poems lurk. And ever since I began to read the *Melody Maker* at the age of fourteen –which told me that racism was active in England –I've been fascinated by the pop charts. They may have more rigging than the *Cutty Sark*, but I can't resist those dramatic leaps to the top, those plunges to the depths, those deadly struggles on the lower rungs.

As a teenager wedged between 1945 and 1952, I was one of the polo-necked minority who spent our money on Bing Crosby, Fats Waller and Hoagy Carmichael. I fell in love with jazz, the blues, rhythm and blues, rock 'n' roll – the words as well as the music:

Baby, you so beautiful, but you gotta die some day –
All I want's a little loving before you pass away.

As Big Joe Turner says, and it may be pretty vulgar, but that music chopped down my heart. Later I spent a year on the lapels of the pop machine, writing a column for the *Daily Mail* in which I introduced the first Top Five chart in a national paper and the first interview with the Beatles too. I've come to realise that I have more in common with Gary Glitter than Rilke.

2. *But how did you choose these poems? I thought you were against beauty contests?*

They're the ones I perform most often and the ones asked for most often. Some of my other poems may be better, but they're less gregarious. There are also some secret poems which are hard to find, hard to understand and only a mother could love them.

3. *All right, then how did you choose the order of your Top Forty?*

I couldn't put my favourite first and my least favourite last or contrariwise, because my feelings about poems change with the weather and my intestinal contraflow. I supposed I could've hired a Clapometer and placed them in order of popularity, but this isn't a bloody game-show, this is big-time Eng. Lit. Look, I may be 'the Frankie Vaughan of Capitalist Verse' (*Sunday Times*), but I got spreads in the *Oxford Companion to English Literature* and the *Cambridge Guide to Ditto*, so leave us cool it. Eventually I decided to imagine I was performing these poems and put them in a good running order.

For a running order I use the old Patchwork Quilt Theory of Structure. Juxtaposition and instinct, compatability and combustibility. A dark square next to a light square. Big poems next to small verses, love poems next to war poems, funny ones next to sad ones. So the best way to read this collection is from the front to the back.

4. *Why the commentaries?*

They're the kind of explanation and footnotes I give during performances, only fuller.

5. *Shouldn't poems stand or fall on their own?*

Maybe they should, but you try telling them. A lot of poems need to have their hands held. Often helps if the audience knows how a poem came to be cooked, or a story which led to it. And there's something very stark about a poetry reading in which one poem follows another with no break. A commentary, especially an improvised commentary, lowers the pressure and gives some breathing space for the poet, the audience and the poems.

6. *Aren't you preaching to the converted?*

This is really a reviewer's question rather than a question I've had from audiences. The Young Tories never invite me to read, so it's seldom that I perform to an audience of utter pagans. But I do perform for all sorts of mixed-up groups – in cabaret, theatre, literary festivals, pubs, prisons and colleges. I read often in primary schools to what is the nearest thing to a cross-section of the classes which you can find in Britain – taking care to preach as little as possible. Those kids aren't converted to anything, but they do have strong imaginations. Some of the worst heckling I've ever had has been at ideologically sympathetic events – from a CND rally in Hyde Park, the London School of Economics and the Ether-Sniffers Table at the Anarchist Ball at the Fulham Town Hall.

7. *Do you consider your audience when writing a poem?*

95 per cent of poets say 'No' to this one in interviews. But I say: 'Yes, somewhere along the line'. I don't start into a poem worrying about who's going to hear it or read it. The first draft, the hot draft, is a scribbled mental free-for-all. No rules, no penalties. Second draft is cooler, a shaping time. Third draft is surgery, the life or death of a thousand cuts. But in the third or fourth draft I do begin to think of my audiences, or rather the lively faces of some faces in that audience – my wife Celia, my good friends Gordon Snell and Albert Hunt, my children all now grown-up. I try to work out if they'll understand what I've written. Otherwise, if I only considered my own understanding, I could write: '24 Rainbow Woods marched on 3 Monkton Combe' and nobody but me would know that 24 is lucky and 3 unlucky, that Rainbow Woods were Heaven to me and Monkton Combe stood for Hell.

A real modernist or post-modernist poet would write about Rainbow Combe 24 times 3 and leave the academics to tease out a meaning during the next two hundred years. I don't want my meanings left to chance quirks of the reader or the mercy of ante-post-structuralist dustheads. I want to speak or sing as clearly as possible to friends and foes alike.

8. *Don't you tend to over-simplify?*

Yes. I'm not a very complicated person, as people go. And they do go, you know. Some of my verses are verbal cartoons. But if I have the choice between clear and simple or cloudy and complex, I go for the glass of water every time. Of course often there's no choice and I find myself in a cloud-maze.

There are hundreds of poets whose work I enjoy, poets of every school and nature. But I'm prejudiced against crossword puzzle poets, disguise poets, acrostic poets and poets who wear balaclavas to conceal their true identities.

11

'Most people ignore most poetry / because / most poetry ignores most people' I wrote at the front of my first book of poems. I meant it, although I did have a secret reason for printing that motto up front – to distract the attention of the poetry reviewers from the poems themselves. It worked. Nearly all of them reviewed the slogan and left my sensitive poems alone. (For more on poetry reviewers, see my commentary to *Adrian Mitchell's Famous Weak Bladder Blues*).

9. Has your writing been affected by all the public readings you've done?

Sure. I've done more than a thousand performances. Sometimes I read a new poem and find there's very little reaction. I don't just mean comments afterwards. I listen to the breathing of an audience, its concentration, its nervousness, its laughs, its sighs, its fidgets and its silences. There may be nothing wrong with the poem, maybe I didn't do well enough. As Mr Beckett says: 'No matter. Try again. Fail again. Fail better.' I try the poem again at my next reading. Again, nothing happens, apart from two people shuffling their knees in stanza three. Afterwards I crawl under the poem and inspect its axles. There you are – a jagged hole in the third stanza, meaning pouring out and down the gutter. I fix the hole, try the poem out on the next audience. Maybe this time it moves. Maybe it still won't start and I'll leave it in the garage until I find time to work on it again, if ever. (But I may well publish it in a book, even if it won't work aloud. I have a poem called 'Autumnobile' of which I'm feverishly fond, but it is guaranteed to turn the cheeriest crowd into sub-zombies. Dunno why, I nicked the shape of it from Pushkin.)

10. Why do you write poems?

I find it hard to talk about the things I care about most, even to my family and friends, and poetry is my way of telling them what I feel. I try to approach an audience as if it's made up of friends, or people who would be my friends if we knew each other. 'No communication is possible except between equals' as *Illuminatus!* teaches us. I write my poems for love – love of language, love of my family, friends and animals, love of the planet, love of life, and I'd be a damned fool if I didn't.

THE TOP 40

Heart on the left
With a hard beat soft beat
Heart on the left
Hits it on the off-beat
Heart on the left
Walking the underdog
Heart on the left
Doing the hedgehog…
SONG IN PROGRESS

When I sing my songs you can't sit still,
your big toe shoot up in your boot.
LITTLE RICHARD

I am not a swan.
BIX BEIDERBECKE

What Is Poetry?
(for Sasho, Daniella, Vladko and Martin Shurbanov)

This happened in Bulgaria – I'm very big in Bulgaria. My best friend there is a poet and lecturer called Sasho Shurbanov. Sasho translates Shakespeare and Milton and me. At my readings in Sofia, to which about nine-tenths of the Bulgarian population flock, Sasho and I do a double act. Before one such performance he warned me that the People of Bulgaria wanted to ask some questions. OK, I said, do you know what they want to ask? Well, this is the main question, he said – What is poetry? Since I didn't have a sensible answer, I wrote a poem. Since then I have contrived various answers including: Poetry is a bucket for holding truth. And: Poetry is truth with a backbeat. I prefer the latter.

Look at those naked words dancing together!
Everyone's very embarrassed.
Only one thing to do about it –
Off with your clothes
And join in the dance.
Naked words and people dancing together.
There's going to be trouble.
Here come the Poetry Police!

Keep dancing.

Song in Space

This was written after seeing the first photos of the planet Earth taken from space, looking very blue and white and beautiful, like my mother. It's a dialogue between a spaceman and the Earth. When I was travelling round England performing during the Falklands Experience I found myself thinking, *Song in Space* is taking on a new meaning – Why are the seas so full of tears? (Because the seas were full of drowning sailors, British and Argentinian.) And then I thought – No, it's the same old meaning, same stupid futile war as usual. And I remembered walking with my friend the composer Peter Schat on some land which had been newly claimed from the sea, a bird sanctuary on a sweet blue day and how I said: Imagine, nobody has ever killed anyone else on this land. And how Peter replied, but when the sea was here, they had plenty of battles above where we're standing.

When man first flew beyond the sky
He looked back into the world's blue eye.
Man said: What makes your eye so blue?
Earth said: The tears in the ocean do.
Why are the seas so full of tears?
Because I've wept so many thousand years.
Why do you weep as you dance through space?
Because I am the mother of the Human Race.

Stufferation

This is a series of riddles. First two lines of each verse forms the riddle, the answer to which is always some material substance like iron or rubber or whatever. Has to be performed with a sort of jazz beat. Roger McGough later wrote his own version with the chorus *I Hate That Stuff*. I like it.

Lovers lie around in it
Broken glass is found in it
Grass
I like that stuff

Tuna fish get trapped in it
Legs come wrapped in it
Nylon
I like that stuff

Eskimos and tramps chew it
Madame Tussaud gave status to it
Wax
I like that stuff

Elephants get sprayed with it
Scotch is made with it
Water
I like that stuff

Clergy are dumbfounded by it
Bones are surrounded by it
Flesh
I like that stuff

Harps are strung with it
Mattresses are sprung with it
Wire
I like that stuff

Carpenters make cots of it
Undertakers use lots of it
Wood
I like that stuff

Cigarettes are lit by it
Pensioners get happy when they sit by it
Fire
I like that stuff

Dankworth's alto is made of it, most of it,
Scoobdidoo is composed of it
Plastic
I like that stuff

Apemen take it to make them hairier
I ate a ton of it in Bulgaria
Yoghurt
I like that stuff

Man-made fibres and raw materials
Old rolled gold and breakfast cereals
Platinum linoleum
I like that stuff

Skin on my hands
Hair on my head
Toenails on my feet
And linen on the bed

Well I like that stuff
Yes I like that stuff
The earth
Is made of earth
And I like that stuff

Song About Mary

The last two lines of the penultimate verse originally read: 'You'd see him arrested at the next sit-down/And he'd raise the poor from the dead'. A Mary also gets into my poem *The Castaways*.

Mary sat on a long brown bench
Reading *Woman's Own* and *She*,
Then a slimy-haired nit with stripes on his collar
Said: 'What's the baby's name to be?'

She looked across to Marks and Spencers
Through the dirty window-pane,
'I think I'll call him Jesus Christ,
It's time he came again.'

The clerk he banged his ledger
And he called the Cruelty Man
Saying: 'This bird thinks she's the mother of Christ,
Do what you bleeding well can.'

They took Mary down to the country
And fed her on country air,
And they put the baby in a Christian home
And he's much happier there.

For if Jesus came to Britain
He would turn its dizzy head,
They'd nail him up on a telegraph pole
Or he'd raise the poor from the dead.

So if you have a little baby
Make sure it's legitimate child,
Bind down his limbs with insurance
And he'll grow up meek and mild
    Meek and mild...meek and mild...meek and mild.

So Don't Feed Your Dog Ordinary Meat,
Feed Him Pal, Pal Meat for Dogs,
P-A-L, Prolongs Active Life
(Enriched with Nourishing
Marrowbone Jelly)

Not only one of the first rock 'n' roll poems, one of the first pop poems too. Around 1958. Should be delivered with hard-rocking fervour, the line in brackets with an echo effect.

My bird had a grin like a water-melon,
My bird was a hopeless case.
She wanted to look like Elvis Presley
So she paid a man to wipe the smile off her face,

He was
My friend the plastic surgeon
Your friend the plastic surgeon
Your friendly neighbourhood plastic surgeon
(Enriched with nourishing marrowbone jelly).

My mate was a dirty little Fascist,
They shouted him down when he cursed the Jews,
And nobody recognised his patriotic motives
Till he hired a man to explain his views,

He got
My friend the public relations man
Your friend the PRO
Your friendly neighbourhood public relations man
(Enriched with nourishing marrowbone jelly).

My dad was a nervy sort of navvy
He insured his job and his life and me,
Fire, flood, suicide and acts of God,
And then he insured his insurance policy,

He paid
My friend the man from the Prudential
Your friend the man from the PRU
Your friendly neighbourhood man from the Prudential
(Enriched with nourishing marrowbone jelly).

My mum spent her life watching telly
Till the Epilogue told her that her soul would burn.
Now she's got peace of mind and she still does nothing
For she pays one-tenth of all we earn

To
My friend the Anglican clergyman
Your friend the clergyman
Your friendly neighbourhood Anglican clergyman
(Enriched with nourishing marrowbone jelly).

The plastic surgeon and the public relations man
The man from the Prudential and the man from God –
Pals, pals, every one a pal.
P-A-L,
Prolongs Active Life
(Enriched with nourishing marrowbone jelly).

Nostalgia – Now Threepence Off

Even the title with its dinosaur *threepence* is nostalgic now. This
was one of the earliest pop poems – around 1958 I guess. (The
Black Power reference is a subsequent rewrite.) As I began to
regress into post-middle age or whatever it's called, I began to
collect more and more of the books I read as a boy. I now have
most of the real titles here, but still lack *The Bumper Fun Book*
and *The Wag's Handbook*. So if you see them, would you let me
know? I remember my mother kneeling on a rubber pad to weed
the borders of her garden at Little Orchard while I sat beside
her on a stool, reading her jokes from *The Wag's Handbook*. She
was a lovely and a patient woman or she would have stabbed me
with her fork.

Where are they now, the heroes of furry-paged books and comics
brighter than life which packed my ink-lined desk in days when
BOP meant *Boys' Own Paper*, where are they anyway?

Where is Percy F Westerman? Where are H.L. Gee and Arthur
Mee? Why is Edgar Rice (*The Warlord of Mars*) Burroughs, the
Bumper Fun Book and the *Wag's Handbook*? Where is the *Wonder
Book of Reptiles*? Where the hell is *The Boy's Book of Bacteriological
Warfare*?

Where are the *Beacon* Readers? Did Ro-ver, that tireless hound,
devour his mon-o-syll-ab-ic-all-y correct family? Did Little Black
Sambo and Epaminondas shout for Black Power?

Did Peter Rabbit get his when myxomatosis came around the
second time, did the Flopsy Bunnies stiffen to a standstill, grow
bug-eyed, fly-covered and then disintegrate?

Where is G.A. Henty and his historical lads – Wolfgang the
Hittite, Armpit the Young Viking, Cyril who lived in Sodom?
Where are their uncorrupted bodies and Empire-building brains,
England needs them, the *Sunday Times* says so.

There is news from the Strewelpeter mob. Johnny-Head-In-Air
spends his days reporting flying saucers, the telephone receiver
never cools from the heat of his hand. Little Harriet, who played
with matches, still burns, but not with fire. The Scissor-man is
everywhere.

Babar the Elephant turned the jungle into a garden city. But things went wrong. John and Susan, Titty and Roger, became unaccountably afraid of water, sold their dinghies, all married each other, live in a bombed-out cinema on surgical spirits and weeds of all kinds.

Snow White was in the *News of the World* – Virgin Lived With Seven Midgets, Court Told. And in the psychiatric ward an old woman dribbles as she mumbles about a family of human bears, they ate porridge, yes Miss Goldilocks of course they did.

Hans Brinker vainly whirled his silver skates round his head as the jackboots of Emil and the Detectives invaded his Resistance Cellar.

Some failed. Desperate Dan and Meddlesome Matty and Strang the Terrible and Korky the Cat killed themselves with free gifts in a back room at the Peter Pan Club because they were impotent, like us. Their audience, the senile Chums of Red Circle School, still wearing for reasons of loyalty and lust the tatters of their uniforms, voted that exhibition a super wheeze.

Some succeeded. Tom Sawyer's heart has cooled, his ingenuity flowers at Cape Kennedy.

But they are all trodden on, the old familiar faces, so at the rising of the sun and the going down of the ditto I remember I remember the house where I was taught to play up play up and play the game though nobody told me what the game was, but we know now, don't we, we know what the game is, but lives of great men all remind us we can make our lives sublime and departing leave behind us arseprints on the sands of time, but the tide's come up, the castles are washed down, where are they now, where are they, where are the deep shelters? There are no deep shelters. Biggles may drop it, Worrals of the Wraf may press the button. So Billy and Bessie Bunter, prepare for the last and cosmic Yarooh and throw away the Man-Tan. The sky will soon be full of suns.

Celia Celia
and
Footnotes on Celia Celia

This was written while I was working for the *Evening Standard*. It became extremely popular, finding its way into all sorts of anthologies. (Once a poem's in one anthology it shoots up the charts – most anthologers only read anthologies.)

It was used in one anthology issued by a florist. They paid me in champagne. But it was also attacked by pirates. Every year *The Guardian* runs pages of Valentines. Readers began to take my poem and adjust its words to suit their own geography:

> When I am sad and weary
> When I think all hope has gone
> When I walk along Billericay High Street (or wherever)
> I think of you...

Just like that, with no thought for the exacting prosodical demands entailed in the re-cutting of one of the crown jewels of twentieth-century English Literature, with no thought but for their steaming bestial desires...hey ho.

PS. I still have the pig, but he has lost his chef's hat and his plastic fried egg and he doesn't work any more. If there is a university archive anywhere which would like to buy a Piggy Cook, would they see me afterwards?

Celia Celia

When I am sad and weary
When I think all hope has gone
When I walk along High Holborn
I think of you with nothing on

Footnotes on Celia Celia

Used to slouch along High Holborn
in my gruesome solo lunch-hours.
It was entirely lined
with Gothick insurance offices
except for one oblong block of a shop
called Gamages,
where, once,
drunk, on Christmas Eve,
I bought myself a battery operated Japanese pig
with a chef's hat on top of his head
and a metal stove which lit up red
and the pig moved a frying pan up and down with his hand
and tossed a plastic fried egg into the air
and caught it again the other way up
and then tossed it and caught it again and again
all the time emitting squeals of excitement
through a series of holes in the top of his head –

but apart from that...I want to forget High Holborn.

Remember Suez?

A History poem. The *Radio Times* used to carry wondrously-drawn advertisements for Officer's Long Combinations. They showed the Officer attempting to look nonchalant, wearing a moustache, his pipe and Officer's Long Combinations. For me he embodied England, totally dignified and totally ridiculous.

England, unlike junior nations,
Wears officers' long combinations.
So no embarrassment was felt
By the Church, the Government or the Crown.
But I saw the Thames like a grubby old belt
And England's trousers falling down.

A Child Is Singing

I was on a long car journey in the front passenger seat with my
niece Ruth, aged four, on my knees. To keep me happy, she sang,
making up her own song as she sang. It lasted for about four
hours and it astonished me through and through. When I got out
of the car I wrote down some of the words as I remembered them.
These form the middle of the poem. I put a three line frame at
either end and there it was. It seemed to me that Ruth could
imagine total destruction far more clearly than most adults.
One of the reasons I like the poem so much is that when it's
read to younger children, they laugh at it.

A child is singing
And nobody listening
But the child who is singing:

Bulldozers grab the earth and shower it.
The house is on fire.
Gardeners wet the earth and flower it.
The house is on fire.
The houses are on fire.
Fetch the fire engine, the fire engine's on fire.
We will have to hide in a hole.
We will burn slow like coal.
All the people are on fire.

And a child is singing
And nobody listening
But the child who is singing.

The Dust

The Dust must have been written about the same time as *A Child Is Singing*, 1956-57. One of my earlier Bomb poems. I write about the Bomb because I dream about the Bomb.

Singing, as she always must,
Like the kitten-drowner with a howling sack,
Open-eyed through the shallow dust
Goes the dust-coloured girl with a child on her back.

    A schoolgirl in a flowered dress,
    Swayed by the swaying of a tree
    And the sun's grin, in front of her family
    One day became a prophetess.

    Like a singer who forgets her song
    She awkwardly leant from the graceful chair,
    Balanced her fists in the drawing-room air
    And said that everyone was wrong, that she was wrong.

    Shocked by this infantile mistake
    Her uncles and aunts were sad to find
    This ugly girl with an ugly mind
    In a house as rich as a birthday cake.

    When the bombs fell, she was sitting with her man,
    Straight and white in the family pew.
    While in her the bud of a child grew
    The city crumbled, the deaths began.

Now, singing as she always must,
A refugee from a love burned black,
Open-eyed through the rising dust
Goes the dust-coloured girl with a child on her back.

Veteran with a Head Wound

Written about 1958. A breakthrough for me. I took it along
with me to my first meeting of The Group, the poets' circle
which met at Edward Lucie-Smith's house. When I read it, people
were very enthusiastic and it was xeroxed to be the main poem
for the following week's meeting. The detailed criticism from
fellow-poets was positive and constructive. Because of it I
changed the title, cut off the first verse and published it in *Delta*.
And my confidence took a huge leap forward. I stopped going to
The Group very soon after. It wasn't boring, but I'd got what I
wanted and so I moved on.

This is an early Green poem, if you like, and must be one of the
first references to acid rain in verse.

Nothing to show for it at first
But dreams and shivering, a few mistakes.
Shapes lounged around his mind chatting of murder,
Telling interminable jokes,
Watching like tourists for Vesuvius to burst.

He started listening. Too engrossed to think,
He let his body move in jerks,
Talked just to prove himself alive, grew thin,
Lost five jobs in eleven weeks,
Then started drinking, blamed it on the drink.

He'd seen a woman, belly tattered, run
Her last yards. He had seen a fat
Friend roll in flames, as if his blood were paraffin,
And herded enemies waiting to be shot
Stand looking straight into the sun.

They couldn't let him rot in the heat
In the corner of England like a garden chair.
A handy-man will take a weathered chair,
Smooth it, lay on a glowing layer
Of paint and tie a cushion to the seat.

They did all anyone could do –
Tried to grate off the colour of his trouble,
Brighten him up a bit. His rare
Visitors found him still uncomfortable.
The old crimson paint showed through.

Each night he heard from the back of his head,
As he was learning to sleep again,
Funny or terrible voices tell
Or ask him how their deaths began.
These are the broadcasts of the dead.

One voice became a plaintive bore,
It could only remember the grain and shine
Of a wooden floor, the forest smell
Of its fine surface. The voice rasped on
For hours about that pretty floor.

'If I could make that floor again,'
The voice insisted, over and over,
'The floor on which I died,' it said,
'Then I could stand on it for ever
Letting the scent of polish lap my brain.'

He became Boswell to the dead.
In cruel script their deaths are written.
Generously they are fed
In that compound for the forgotten,
His crowded, welcoming head.

The doctors had seen grimmer cases.
They found his eyes were one-way mirrors,
So they could easily look in
While he could only see his terrors,
Reflections of those shuttered faces.

Stepping as far back as I dare,
(For the man may stagger and be broken
Like a bombed factory or hospital),
I see his uniform is woven
Of blood, bone, flesh and hair.

Populated by the simple dead,
This soldier, in his happy dreams,
Is killed before he kills at all.
Bad tenant that he is, I give him room;
He is the weeper in my head.

Since London's next bomb will tear
Her body in its final rape,
New York and Moscow's ashes look the same
And Europe go down like a battleship,
Why should one soldier make me care?

Ignore him or grant him a moment's sadness.
He walks the burning tarmac road
To the asylum built with bricks of flame.
Abandon him and you must make your own
House of incinerating madness.

The horizon is only paces away.
We walk an alley through a dark,
Criminal city. None can pass.
We would have to make love, fight or speak
If we met someone travelling the other way.

A tree finds its proportions without aid.
Dogs are not tutored to be fond.
Penny-size frogs traverse the grass
To the civilisation of a pond.
Grass withers yearly, is re-made.

Trees become crosses because man is born.
Dogs may be taught to shrink from any hand.
Dead frogs instruct the scientist;
Spread clouds of poison in the pond –
You kill their floating globes of spawn.

In London, where the trees are lean,
The banners of the grass are raised.
Grass feeds the butcher and the beast,
But we could conjure down a blaze
Would scour the world of the colour green.

For look, though the human soul is tough,
Our state scratches itself in bed
And a thousand are pierced by its fingernails.
It combs its hair, a thousand good and bad
Fall away like discs of dandruff.

For a moment it closes its careful fist
And, keening for the world of streets,
More sons of god whisper in jails
Where the unloved the unloved meet.
The days close round them like a dirty mist.

When death covers England with a sheet
Of red and silver fire, who'll mourn the state,
Though some will live and some bear children
And some of the children born in hate
May be both lovely and complete?

Try to distract this soldier's mind
From his distraction. Under the powdered buildings
He lies alive, still shouting,
With his brothers and sisters and perhaps his children,
While we bury all the dead people we can find.

Icarus Shmicarus

Supposed to be spoken by somebody with power to somebody in their power – a jailer to a prisoner, teacher to a child, man to a woman – or vice versa.

Peter Brook used it in his *US* but didn't like the lines 'If you lick the boots that kick you/then you'll never feel the lash'. After a ridiculous lunchtime in a pub inventing alternatives with Dick Peaslee, the composer, I came up with 'If you build your house of garbage/then you'll love the smell of trash' which I offered as a joke but Peter accepted as a gem. Taught me something.

If you never spend your money
you know you'll always have some cash.
If you stay cool and never burn
you'll never turn to ash.
If you lick the boots that kick you
then you'll never feel the lash,
and if you crawl along the ground
at least you'll never crash.
So why why why –
WHAT MADE YOU THINK YOU COULD FLY?

B

To You

Peace Is Milk was written shortly after my one and only break-down. This was written just before, as a personal note to my wife Celia to explain what was running through my head in hobnail boots. I thought it was a very private poem. But then I took the risk of reading it in public and found that it always brought a special response, there were always people, not necessarily my generation, who'd been through similar troubles. What I thought was one of my most personal poems became one of my most public, especially when Peter Schat the Dutch composer set it to music and performed it in concert.

Later my fear of madness receded until nowadays it stands at only number 29 on my hit list of Fears.

One: we were swaddled, ugly-beautiful and drunk on milk.
Two: cuddled in arms always covered by laundered sleeves.
Three: we got sand and water to exercise our imaginative faculties.
Four: we were hit. Suddenly hit.

Five: we were fed to the educational system limited.
Six: worried by the strange creatures in our heads, we strangled
         some of them.
Seven: we graduated in shame.
Eight: World War Two and we hated the Germans as much as
         our secret bodies, loved the Americans as much as the Russians,
         hated killing, loved killing, depending on the language in the Bible
         in the breast pocket of the dead soldier, we were crazy-thirsty
         for Winston Superman, for Jesus with his infinite tommy-gun
         and the holy Spitfires, while the Jap dwarfs hacked through the
         undergrowth of our nightmares – there were pits full of people-
         meat – and the real bombs came, but they didn't hit us, my love,
         they didn't hit us exactly.
My love, they are trying to drive us mad.

So we got to numbers eight, nine, ten, and eleven,
growing scales over every part of our bodies,
Especially our eyes,

Because scales were being worn, because scales were armour.
And now we stand, past thirty, together, madder than ever,
We make a few diamonds and lose them.
We sell our crap by the ton.
My love, they are trying to drive us mad.

Make love. We must make love
Instead of making money.
You know about rejection? Hit. Suddenly hit.
Want to spend my life building poems in which untamed
People and animals walk around freely, lie down freely
Make love freely
In the deep loving carpets, stars circulating in their ceilings,
Poems like honeymoon planetariums.
But our time is burning.
My love, they are trying to drive us mad.

Peace was all I ever wanted.
It was too expensive.
My love, they are trying to drive us mad.

Half the people I love are shrinking.
My love, they are trying to drive us mad.

Half the people I love are exploding.
My love, they are trying to drive us mad.

I am afraid of going mad.

C'mon Everybody

Dedicated to Chubby Checker. Note for the young: Chubby Checker was a prophet who came unto England and he said unto the English: 'Behold – the pelvis!' And the English said: 'Right, Chubby.' And Chubby said unto them: 'Lo, the pelvis is a moveable part.' And the English said unto him: 'Chubby, thou kiddest.' But Chubby did Twist in the sight of the English people and soon the population of the archipelago was moving and grooving and that's probably how and when and why you got born. Well, after the Twist came the Mashed Potato and we did it, and the Fly and we tried it and the Dog – we were embarrassed but we had a stab at it. But then Chubby seemed to run out of dance and hits and I wanted to advance his career as well as that of Western Civilisation so I wrote this one about a dance I was brought up to do and that most people all around me seemed to be doing and here it is – and a very early example of rock 'n' roll poetry it is.

There's a grand old dance that's rockin the nation
Shake your money and shut your mouth
Taking the place of copulation
S'called The Bourgeois.

See that girl with the diamond thing?
Shake your money and shut your mouth
Didn't get that by picketing
She done The Bourgeois

Do-gooder, do-gooder where you been?
Shake your money and shut your mouth
Done myself good, got a medal from the Queen
For The Bourgeois.

Is it a singer? *No.*
Is it a lover? *No.*
Is it a bourgeois? *Yeaaah!*

Wave your missile around the vault
Shake your money and shut your mouth
Somebody suffers well it ain't your fault
That you're Bourgeois.

I play golf so I exist
Shake your money and shut your mouth
Eye on the ball and hand over fist
I do The Bourgeois.

Five days a week on the nine-eleven
Shake your money and shut your mouth
When we die we'll go to Bournemouth
Cos we're Bourgeois.

The Liberal Christ Gives a Press Conference

Used to be called *The Liberal Christ Gives an Interview* – but I
found it much more lively to cast the audience as representatives
of the media and myself, natch, as the Naz. To avoid death threats,
I should point put that this is a liberal version of JC speaking,
not the real (Sylvesterised) McCoy, who was a rabble-rousing
conchie of the first water.
    I used to be a Christian way back, and my evangelical teachers
taught me the fear of Hell and the dread of the human body. I'm
still in favour of Jesus, among many others, but as for his churches
– what we need is a cosmic waste disposal unit.

I would have walked on the water
But I wasn't fully insured.
And the BMA sent a writ my way
With the very first leper I cured.

I would've preached a golden sermon
But I didn't like the look of the Mount.
And I would've fed fifty thousand
But the Press wasn't there to count.

    And the businessmen in the temple
    Had a team of coppers on the door.
    And if I'd spent a year in the desert
    I'd have lost my pension for sure.

    I would've turned the water into wine
    But they weren't giving licences.
    And I would have died and been crucified
    But like – you know how it is.

    I'm going to shave off my beard
    And cut my hair,
    Buy myself some bulletproof
    Underwear
    I'm the Liberal Christ
    And I've got no blood to spare.

The Oxford Hysteria of English Poetry

I spent three years at Oxford studying Modern English Literature (500-1815). Allegedly. So I thought I should pass on the fruits of my enhanced brainbox to all and sundry especially the latter. Most of my audience is pretty sundry. It is meant to be spoken by a very old battered poet who has survived from the days when we had pterodactyls instead of critics. For this edition only I have added an exclusive verse about some of my mates from Liverpool. I am quite often described as a Liverpool poet myself because I was born in London and have lived in Surrey, Somerset, Cardiff, Cambridge, Iowa City, Oxford, Connecticut, Suffolk, Devon and the Yorkshire Dales. (Note for the worried: Adrian Henri is the Liverpool Adrian. Anyway I've worked in Liverpool and I love the city and many of its inmates and exiles, so I'm happy either way.)

Back in the caveman days business was fair.
Used to turn up at Wookey Hole,
Plenty of action down the Hole
Nights when it wasn't raided.
They'd see my bear-gut harp
And the mess at the back of my eyes
And 'Right,' they'd say, 'make poetry,'
So I'd slam away at the three basic chords
And go into the act –
A story about the sabre-toothed tigers with a comic hero,
A sexy one with an anti-wife clubbing twist –
Good progressive stuff mainly,
Get ready for the Bronze Age, all that.
And soon it would be 'Bring out the woad!'
Yeah, woad. We used to get high on woad.

The Vikings only wanted sagas
Full of gigantic deadheads cutting off each other's vitals
Or Beowulf Versus the Bog People.
The Romans weren't much better
Under all that armour you could tell they were soft

With their central heating
And poets with names like Horace.

Under the Normans the language began to clear
Became a pleasure to write in,
Yes, write in, by now everyone was starting
To write down poems.
Well, it saved memorising and improvising
And the peasants couldn't get hold of it.
Soon there were hundreds of us
Most of us writing under the name
Of Geoffrey Chaucer.

Then suddenly we were knee-deep in sonnets.
Holinshed ran a headline:
BONANZA FOR BARDS.
It got fantastic –
Looning around from the bear-pit to the Globe,
All those freak-outs down the Mermaid,
Kit Marlowe coming on like Richard the Two,
A virgin Queen in a ginger wig
And English poetry in full whatsit –
Bloody fantastic, but I never found any time
To do any writing till Willy finally flipped –
Smoking too much of the special stuff
Sir Walter Raleigh was pushing.

Cromwell's time I spent on cultural committees.

Then Charles the Second swung down from the trees
And it was sexual medley time
And the only verses they wanted
Were epigrams on Chloë's breasts
But I only got published on the back of her left knee-cap.

Next came Pope and Dryden
So I went underground.
Don't mess with the Mafia.

Then suddenly – WOOMF –
It was the Ro-man-tic Re-viv-al
And it didn't matter how you wrote,

All the public wanted was a hairy great image.
Before they'd even print you
You had to smoke opium, die of consumption,
Fall in love with your sister
And drown in the Mediterranean (not at Brighton).
My publisher said: 'I'll have to remainder you
Unless you go and live in a lake or something
Like this bloke Wordsworth.'

After that there were about
A thousand years of Tennyson
Who got so bored with himself
That he changed his name
To Kipling at half-time.

Strange that Tennyson should be
Remembered for his poems really,
We always thought of him
As a golfer.

There hasn't been much time
For poetry since the Twenties
What with leaving the Communist Church
To join the Catholic Party
And explaining why in the *CIA Monthly*.
In 1963, for one night only,
I became the fourth Liverpool Marx Brother.
There was Groucho McGough,
Chico Henri, Harpo Patten
And me, I was Zeppo,
Yer, I was Pete Best.
Finally I was given the Chair of Comparative Ambiguity
At Armpit University, Java.
It didn't keep me busy,
But it kept me quiet.
It seemed like poetry had been safely tucked up for the night.

Norman Morrison

This was written based on the first newspaper reports. Later I investigated Norman Morrison's life and death in much more detail, especially when working on Peter Brook's *US*. Morrison's death moved many people, especially the North Vietnamese, who were amazed that an American could care so much for their suffering.

I remember being called on to read this in Trafalgar Square when I had just noticed that, down below the platform, and out of sight of 98 per cent of the crowd, people were being forced forward into the arms of a police line, pulled individually past the line, and beaten with truncheons while their coats were pulled over their heads. I just kept reading the poem at the police, trying to calm them, reading slow. I don't think it helped, but I didn't know what else to do. If I'd told the crowd exactly what was happening there could well have been deaths, on both sides.

On November 2nd 1965
in the multi-coloured multi-minded
United beautiful States of terrible America
Norman Morrison set himself on fire
outside the Pentagon.
He was thirty-one, he was a Quaker,
and his wife (seen weeping in the newsreels)
and his three children
survive him as best they can.
He did it in Washington where everyone could see
because
people were being set on fire
in the dark corners of Vietnam where nobody could see.
Their names, ages, beliefs and loves
are not recorded.
This is what Norman Morrison did.
He poured petrol over himself.
He burned. He suffered.
He died.
That is what he did
in the heart of Washington

where everyone could see.
He simply burned away his clothes,
his passport, his pink-tinted skin,
put on a new skin of flame
and became
Vietnamese.

Fifteen Million Plastic Bags

I worked on the *Evening Standard* Londoner's Diary for a couple
of years with a cheerful band of young reporters, most of us wear-
ing CND badges and most of us involved in crumbling marriages.
One day we were sent a story saying that the government had
ordered fifteen million plastic bags for corpse disposal in case of
a nuclear misunderstanding. I was put on this case, but could get
nothing but denials from the Ministry of Defence, Home Office
and ICI. So we couldn't run the story in the paper. But that didn't
stop me making a poem or rather, a song. I wrote it to the tune of
St James Infirmary and my daughter Sasha sometimes sings it. I
sent it to Ned Sherrin at *That Was The Week That Was*, but he
said it was too much like a Protest Song. I said it was a Protest
Song. And it still is.

I was walking in a government warehouse
Where the daylight never goes.
I saw fifteen million plastic bags
Hanging in a thousand rows.

Five million bags were six feet long
Five million were five foot five
Flve million were stamped with Mickey Mouse
And they came in a smaller size.

Were they for guns or uniforms
Or a dirty kind of party game?
Then I saw each bag had a number
And every bag bore a name.

And five million bags were six feet long
Five million were five foot five
Five million were stamped with Mickey Mouse
And they came in a smaller size.

So I've taken my bag from the hanger
And I've pulled it over my head
And I'll wait for the priest to zip it
So the radiation won't spread.

Now five million bags are six feet long
Five million are five foot five
Five million are stamped with Mickey Mouse
And they come in a smaller size.

You Get Used To It

I read two poems at the Albert Hall rave-up in 1965. This was the first. The other was *To Whom It May Concern*. Originally the second verse featured a 'half crown book of nudes'. Then it became 50p. I don't know how much they cost these days, do you?

'Am I in Alabama or am I in hell?'
A minister, Montgomery, Alabama, March 1965

Begging-bowl eyes, begging-bowl eyes,
skin round hoops of wire.
They do not eat, they are been eaten,
saw them in the papers.

But it's only bad if you know it's bad,
fish don't want the sky.
If you've spent all your life in hell or Alabama
you get used to it.

Ignorant husband, ignorant wife,
each afraid of the other one's bomb.
He spends all he has in the Gentlemen's
on a 50p book of nudes.

But it's only bad if you know it's bad,
fish don't want the sky.
If you've spent all your life in hell or Alabama
you get used to it.

Beautiful blossom of napalm
sprouting from the jungle,
bloom full of shrivelling things,
might be mosquitoes, might be men.

But it's only bad if you know it's bad,
fish don't want the sky.
If you've spent all your life in hell or Alabama
you get used to it.

I hurt, you hurt, he hurts, she hurts,
we hurt, you hurt, they hurt.
What can't be cured must go to jail,
what can't be jailed must die.

   But it's only bad if you know it's bad,
   fish don't want the sky.
   If you've spent all your life in hell or Alabama
   you get used to it.

To Whom It May Concern

Probably my most notorious poem, often known as *Tell Me Lies About Vietnam*, this was inspired by hearing Bernard Levin, on a TV show, explaining why British troops should be sent to Vietnam to support our American allies. At the time, early 1965, this seemed a very real possibility.

I think I first read it at an anti-war rally. My old friend Peter O'Toole read it, with a golden trumpet for a voice, in Trafalgar Square, after working on it for hours and hours. I performed it at the famous 1965 poetry reading when 7000 freaks packed the Albert Hall. The response was enormous.

It was not and never has been a poem about the Vietnam war. I've never been to Vietnam. It was a poem about sitting comfortably in a safe country and sometimes wishing that the news of the murderous world would stop. About the times when we wish to be cut off from the truth. But a poem about the necessity for the truth.

It has been parodied and attacked in verse. It was set to music by Richard Peaslee and used as a recurring theme in Peter Brook's *US* and his movie *Tell Me Lies*. I asked Spike Milligan if I could perform it on his TV show because I wanted to do it on TV and couldn't think of anyone else who'd let me. Spike's producer said I could only do it if I took a custard pie in the face at the end, like everyone else in the show. I've always loved custard pies, so that was great. I was allowed to perform it on BBC Radio's *Books, Plays and Poems* programme – but only after some nameless suitocrat had insisted that it be checked with the Foreign Office. The F.O. chap said it was OK to broadcast, in fact he thought it was a pretty good poem. A real gent.

I was run over by the truth one day.
Ever since the accident I've walked this way
    So stick my legs in plaster
    Tell me lies about Vietnam.

Heard the alarm clock screaming with pain,
Couldn't find myself so I went back to sleep again
    So fill my ears with silver
    Stick my legs in plaster
    Tell me lies about Vietnam.

Every time I shut my eyes all I see is flames.
Made a marble phone book and I carved all the names
    So coat my eyes with butter
    Fill my ears with silver
    Stick my legs in plaster
    Tell me lies about Vietnam.

I smell something burning, hope it's just my brains.
They're only dropping peppermints and daisy-chains
    So stuff my nose with garlic
    Coat my eyes with butter
    Fill my ears with silver
    Stick my legs in plaster
    Tell me lies about Vietnam.

Where were you at the time of the crime?
Down by the Cenotaph drinking slime
    So chain my tongue with whisky
    Stuff my nose with garlic
    Coat my eyes with butter
    Fill my ears with silver
    Stick my legs in plaster
    Tell me lies about Vietnam.

You put your bombers in, you put your conscience out,
You take the human being and you twist it all about
    So scrub my skin with women
    Chain my tongue with whisky
    Stuff my nose with garlic
    Coat my eyes with butter
    Fill my ears with silver
    Stick my legs in plaster
    Tell me lies about Vietnam.

Adrian Mitchell's Famous Weak Bladder Blues

It's time to pay tribute to the poetry reviewers of Britain. They have been very helpful to me in my work. They have often imparted to me good advice like: 'Don't write about war, Adrian. Leave war to Generals. And don't write about politics – leave that to the Houses of Parliament. Don't write about religion – we've got churches for that.' And I answered unto them and said: 'All right, poetry reviewers of Britain, I won't write about war, politics or religion – but what would you like me to write about?' And a couple of the PROB replied, saying: 'Well, you have written, just occasionally, about your own personal pain, and those poems seem more successful than your public ones, so why don't you concentrate on your own personal pain, yes, give us some of that inner anguish, that's what we're really slavering for...' So I thought unto myself, well I haven't had that much personal pain in my life, I've had enough I guess, but I was born white, middle class, British, near Hampstead Heath, I've had less than my share of personal pain look at it globally – and then it struck me – my Disability? Ever since I left the pram, my life has been shaped by the need never to enter a strange area without mentally mapping the swiftest route to the Gents. As a student I found drinking beer meant that I missed half of any given conversation. But if I was frequent, at least I was bloody quick. So I thought I'd exploit my Personal Pain and, in a cottage above Betws-y-Coed, composed this lump of literature. I put 'Famous' in the title in order to help these versicles become world renowned. Didn't work. But they are dedicated to my paramedics – the good old PROBs.

Now some praise God because he gave us the bomb to drop in 1945
But I thank the Lord for equipping me with the fastest cock alive.

You may think a sten-gun's frequent, you can call greased lightning
    fast,
But race them down to the Piccadilly bog and watch me zooming
    past.

Well it's excuse me,
And I'll be back.
Door locked so rat-a-tat-tat.
You mind if I go first?
I'm holding this cloudburst.
I'll be out in 3.7 seconds flat.

I've got the Adamant Trophy, the Niagara Cup, you should see me
        on the M1 run,
For at every comfort station I've got a reputation for – doing the ton.

Once I met that Speedy Gonzales and he was first through the
        door.
But I was unzipped, let rip, zipped again and out before he could
        even draw.

Now God killed John Lennon and he let Barry Manilow survive,
But the good Lord blessed little Adrian Mitchell with the fastest
        cock alive.

Peace Is Milk

Back in the very early 60s I ran into a minor breakdown. I'd been working for years without a holiday it seemed and was horribly tired. One day I started crying and found that I simply couldn't stop. My wife Celia found out from friends about a doctor/psychiatrist called Sydney Gottlieb, one of the kindest and wisest people I ever met. He asked me the hard question which I think he puts to most of his patients: 'What do you want?' After some evasion I managed to tell him, between my sobs: 'I want to sleep for a week. But not in a hospital.' So he fixed that. I slept for a week, with the help of injections, at our friend Trix Craig's house. Sydney talked to my newspaper and told them I needed a month's holiday. We had no money for a holiday. Writers help writers. Troy and Diana Kennedy Martin lent us their house in the South of France for a month. David Mercer lent us the money for a holiday. Celia took me out, lay me down in the sun and turned me over every time there was a smell of burning. I recovered. Sydney talked with me again, explained that I was so run down partly because I took no exercise. I listened. He saved my life.

While I was doing my famous Sleep For A Week I was given vitamin injections, pieces of cheese and milk. Towards the end of the week, when I was coming round, the phrase formed in my mind – *Peace Is Milk*. When I returned to writing, it became the starting point of a long poem. The acid in the poem is not lysergic acid, whatever the *Times Literary Supplement* thinks.

I've been asked several times, why elephants? Because I like elephants. Because they are strong and gentle. Because thanks to a seven-year course at Elephant Drawing College, I can draw them. Because they are there.

Peace is milk.
War is acid.
The elephant dreams of bathing in lakes of milk.
Acid blood
Beats through the veins
Of the monstrous, vulture-weight fly,
Shaking, rocking his framework.

The elephants, their gentle thinking shredded
By drugs disseminated in the electricity supply,
Sell their children, buy tickets for the Zoo
And form a dead-eyed queue
Which stretches from the decorative, spiked gates
To the enormous shed where the flies are perching.

Peace is milk
War is acid.
Sometimes an elephant finds a bucket of milk.
Swash! and it's empty.
The fly feeds continually.
The fly bulges with acid
Or he needs more. And more.

An overweight fly levers himself
From his revolving chair,
Paces across the elephantskin floor,
Presses a button
And orders steak, steak, elephant steak
And a pint of acid.

Peace is milk.
War is acid.
The elephants are being dried in the sun.
The huge flies overflow.

Look down from the plane.
Those clouds of marvellous milk.
Easily they swing by on the wind,
Assembling, disassembling,
Forming themselves into pleasure-towers,
Unicorns, waterfalls, funny faces;
Swimming, basking, dissolving –
Easily, easily.

Tomorrow the cream-clouds will be fouled.
The sky will be buckshot-full of paratroop swarms
With their money-talking guns,
Headlines carved across their foreheads,
Sophisticated, silent electrical equipment,
Heart-screws and fear-throwers.

The day after tomorrow
The clouds will curdle, the clouds will begin to burn –
Yes, we expected that, knew about that,
Overkill, overburn, multi-megacorpse,
Yeah, yeah, yeah we knew about that
Cry the white-hearted flies.

Channel One –
A fly scientist in an ivory helmet
Who always appears about to cry
Explains why the viewers have to die.

Channel Nine –
A fly statesman,
Hardly audible through the acid rain,
Explains why nothing can ever happen again.

Oh we'll soon be finished with the creatures of the earth.
There's no future in elephants, milk or Asiatics.
We should be working out
How to inflict the maximum pain
On Martians and Venusians.

Sour sky.
The elephants are entering the shed.
Sour sky.
The flies have dropped a star called Wormwood
And turned the Pacific into an acid bath.
Sour sky.
Socrates said no harm could come to a good man,
But even Socrates
Couldn't turn the hemlock into a banana milk-shake
With one high-voltage charge
From his Greek-sky eyes.
Even Socrates, poor bugger.

They are rubbing their forelegs together,
Washing each others' holes with their stubbled tongues,
Watching us while they wash.
Then like brown rain running backwards,
They hurtle upwards, vibrating with acid.
They patrol our ceilings, always looking downwards.

Pick up the phone, that's them buzzing.
The turd-born flies.

Peace is milk
And milk is simple
And milk is hard to make.
It takes clean grass, fed by clean earth, clear air, clean rain,
Takes a calm cow with all her stomachs working
And it takes milk to raise that cow.

The milk is not for the good elephant.
The milk is not for the bad elephant.
But the milk may be for the lucky elephant
Looming along until the end of the kingdom of the flies.

A family of people, trapped in Death Valley,
Drank from the radiator,
Laid out the hubcaps as bowls for the dew,
Buried each other up to the neck in sand
And waited for better times, which came
Just after they stopped hoping.

So the sweet survival of the elephants demands
Vision, cunning, energy and possibly burial
Until, maybe, the good times roll for the first time
And a tidal wave of elephants,
A stampede of milk,
Tornadoes through the capitals of flydom,
Voices flow like milk,
And below the white, nourishing depths –
Bodies moving any way they want to move,
Eyes resting or dancing at will,
Limbs and minds which follow, gladly,
The music of the milk.

So you drink my milk, I'll drink yours.
We'll melt together in the sun
Despite the high-explosive flies
Which hover, which hover,
Which hover, which hover,
Like a million plaguey Jehovahs.

Their prisons, their police, their armies, their laws,
Their camps where Dobermans pace the cadaver of a field,
Their flame factories and Black Death Factories,
The sourness of their sky –
Well that's the poisonous weather the elephants must lumber through,
Surviving, surviving,
Until the good times roll for the first time.

But it doesn't end
With an impregnable city carved out of the living light.
It doesn't end
In the plastic arms of an Everest-size Sophia Loren.
It doesn't end
When the world says a relieved farewell to the white man
As he goofs off to colonise the Milky Way.

It continues, it continues.
When all of the elephants push it goes slowly forward.
When they stop pushing it rolls backwards.
It continues, it continues.
Towards milk, towards acid.

The taste of milk has been forgotten.
Most elephants agree peace is impossible.
Choosing death instead, they are jerked towards death
Slowly by newspapers, nightmares or cancer,
More quickly by heroin or war.
And some, the tops of their skulls sliced off
By money-knives or the axes of guilt,
Bow their great heads and let their hurting brains
Slop in the lavatory to drown.

There are prophets like Ginsberg – grandson of William Blake –
Desperate elephants who drink a pint of diamonds.
Their eyes become scored with a thousand white trenches,
Their hide shines with a constellation
Of diamond-headed boils,
Each footstep leaves a pool of diamond dust.
And sure, they shine,
They become shouting stars,
Burning with light until they are changed by pain
Into diamonds for everyone.

And sure, they go down shining,
They shine themselves to death,
The diamond drinkers.

The world is falling to pieces
But some of the pieces taste good.

There are various ways of making peace,
Most of them too childish for English elephants.
Given time and love it's possible
To cultivate a peace-field large enough
For the playing of one child.
It's possible to prepare a meal
And give it with care and love
To someone who takes it with care and love.
These are beginnings, but it's late, late –
TV Dinner tonight.
It's possible to suck the taste of peace
From one blade of grass
or recognise peace in a can of white paint,
But it's not enough.
In Nirvana there's only room for one at a time.

WELL, YOU COULD STOP KILLING PEOPLE FOR A START.

Let loose the elephants.
Let the fountains talk milk.
Free the grass, let it walk wherever it likes.
Let the passports and prisons burn, their smoke turning into milk.
Let the pot-smokers blossom into milk-coloured mental petals.
We all need to be breast-fed
And start again.

Tear the fly-woven lying suits
Off the backs of the white killers
And let their milky bodies
Make naked pilgrimage
To wash the sores of Africa and Asia
With milk, for milk is peace
And money tastes of guns,
Guns taste of acid.

Make love well, generously, deeply.
There's nothing simpler in the savage world,
Making good love, making good good love.
There's nothing harder in the tender world,
Making good love, making good good love,
And most of the elephants, most of the time
Go starving for good love, not knowing what the pain is,
But it can be done and thank Blake it is done,
Making good love, making good good love
In houses built of fly-turds, in fly-turd feasting mansions,
Fly-fear insurance offices even,
Fly-worshipping cathedrals even,
Even in murder offices just off the corridors of fly-power –
Making good love, making good good love.

Good lovers float.
Happy to know they are becoming real.
They float out and above the sourness, high on the seeds of peace.
There are too few of them up here.
Too little milk.
Drink more milk.
Breed more cows and elephants.
Think more milk and follow your banana.
We need evangelist, door-to-door lovers,
Handing it out, laying it down,
Spreading the elephant seed, delivering the revolutionary milk,
Making good love, making good good love.
United Nations teams of roving elephant milkmen
Making good love, making good good love,
Because peace is milk,
Peace is milk
And the skinny, thirsty earth, its face covered with flies,
Screams like a baby.

Back in the Playground Blues

When I was nine or ten I spent a couple of years in a school in Hell.
It was a preparatory school in Somerset. I was a day-boy, but not
a "natural victim". According to the class poll I was second most
popular boy in the class. But that was no protection against bullies.
We were left to ourselves much of the time, in the classroom and
in the playground. We – the smaller boys – were tortured every
day by the bigger boys. The only future seemed to lie in growing
bigger and becoming a torturer. Finally I gave up, walked home
and told my mother I'd never go back. She asked why and was
shocked and angry when she found out about the bullying. Within
weeks I was on my way to Greenways, a small boarding school
where bullying was almost unknown. My teacher there told me
recently that when I arrived I was still white and shaking.

I wouldn't have written this poem if I wasn't very aware that
bullying still goes on, especially in enormous schools with enor-
mous classes. Schools where kids are scared to walk the corridors
alone. What's the answer? Smaller schools – 300 kids maximum.
Smaller classes – twelve kids to a teacher, though even Jesus had
problems. No unsupervised areas in schools. When England has
achieved that, I will give some more advice about education.

I dreamed I was back in the playground, I was about four feet high
Yes dreamed I was back in the playground, standing about four
        feet high
Well the playground was three miles long and the playground was
        five miles wide

It was broken black tarmac with a high wire fence all around
Broken black dusty tarmac with a high fence running all around
And it had a special name to it, they called it The Killing Ground

Got a mother and a father, they're one thousand years away
The rulers of The Killing Ground are coming out to play
Everybody thinking: 'Who they going to play with today?'

Well you get it for being Jewish
And you get it for being black
Get it for being chicken
And you get it for fighting back
You get it for being big and fat
Get it for being small
Oh those who get it get it and get it
For any damn thing at all

Sometimes they take a beetle, tear off its six legs one by one
Beetle on its black back, rocking in the lunchtime sun
But a beetle can't beg for mercy, a beetle's not half the fun

I heard a deep voice talking, it had that iceberg sound
'It prepares them for Life' – but I have never found
Any place in my life worse than The Killing Ground.

Leaflets
(for Brian Patten and my twelve students at Bradford)

This was written one day in the sunny Sixties after spending several hours handing out Anti-Apartheid leaflets in Hampstead High Street, not one of my more dangerous missions. It's been a rewarding piece, since several students have told me they used it as a basis for performance pieces which they enjoyed.

My twelve students in Bradford were at Bradford College of Art, where Albert Hunt employed me to invent projects. These twelve worked with me on the first group-written show I ever initiated. Called *Bradford Walk* it was a re-enactment of a bus journey and country walk which culminated in a party and a shower of gifts for the audience. Few of the students had written for fun before, but they all made good warm poems and songs for that show, one of the happiest moments of my life.

Outside the plasma supermarket
I stretch out my arm to the shoppers and say:
'Can I give you one of these?'

I give each of them a leaf from a tree.

The first shopper thanks me.
The second puts the leaf in his mack pocket where his wife won't see.
The third says she is not interested in leaves. She looks like a
    mutilated willow.
The fourth says 'Is it art?' I say that it is a leaf.
The fifth looks through his leaf and smiles at the light beyond.
The sixth hurls down his leaf and stamps it till dark purple mud
    oozes through.
The seventh says she will press it in her album.
The eighth complains that it is an oak leaf and says he would be on
    my side if I were also handing out birch leaves, apple leaves,
    privet leaves and larch leaves.
I say that it is a leaf.
The ninth takes the leaf carefully and then, with a backhand fling,
    gives it its freedom.
It glides, following surprise curving alleys through the air.

It lands. I pick it up.
The tenth reads both sides of the leaf twice and then says: 'Yes,
	but it doesn't say who we should kill.'

But you took your leaf like a kiss.

They tell me that, on Saturdays,
You can be seen in your own city centre
Giving away forests, orchards, jungles.

Saw It in the Papers

In *The Guardian*, as a matter of fact. I was working on a short-lived TV arts programme called *Full House*. I was supposed to be writing sketches about the arts, but after I read this story I asked if I could write a reaction to it as my contribution to the week's programme. Because the story shocked me so much and so many people so much and I wanted to try and understand the woman in the centre of it through writing about her. I tried – I wrote it, I broadcast it, and *The Guardian* published it, together with my explanatory note. My friend Gaie Houston contributed to it after the first draft, helping me to find the key line about unlocking locked-up love.

More than a hundred letters arrived as a result, most of them sympathetic, many from people who wanted to help people in prison. I answered their letters, giving them addresses of organisations etc. With my wife, I visited the woman concerned in prison and we helped her as much as we could.

I try to read poems in prisons when I'm invited. There's no hungrier audience, no more rewarding audience. I read this poem in Gloucester prison. In Victorian times each man had one cell for the night and another for the day. When I visited it they had three men in the day cell and three in the night – that is six men where the Victorians had one. The two verses beginning *There is love in prisons* were written in direct response to a speech made by a member of that audience. It's a piece which I've rewritten many times since it was published. Poetry doesn't have to be a one-man band.

Her baby was two years old.
She left him, strapped in his pram, in the kitchen.
She went out.
She stayed with friends.
She went out drinking.

The baby was hungry.
Nobody came.
The baby cried.

Nobody came.
The baby tore at the upholstery of his pram.
Nobody came.

She told the police:
'I thought the neighbours would hear him crying,
and report it to someone who would come
and take him away.'

Nobody came.

The baby died of hunger.

She said she'd arranged for a girl,
whose name she couldn't remember,
to come and look after the baby
while she stayed with friends.
Nobody saw the girl.
Nobody came.

Her lawyer said there was no evidence
of mental instability.
But the man who promised to marry her
went off with another woman.

And when he went off, this mother changed
from a mother who cared for her two-year-old baby
into a mother who did not seem to care at all.
There was no evidence of mental instability.

The Welfare Department spokesman said:
'I do not know of any plans for an inquiry.
We never become deeply involved.'
Nobody came.
There was no evidence of mental instability.

When she was given love
She gave love freely to her baby.
When love was torn away from her
she locked her love away.
It seemed that no one cared for her.
She seemed to stop caring.
Nobody came.
There was no evidence of mental instability.

Only love can unlock locked-up-love.

Manslaughter: She pleaded Guilty.
She was sentenced to be locked up
in prison for four years.

Is there any love in prisons?

She must have been in great pain.

There is love in prisons.
There is great love in prisons.
A man in Gloucester Prison told me:
'Some of us care for each other.
Some of us don't.
Some of us are gentle,
Some are brutal.
All kinds.'

I said: 'Just the same as people outside.'
He nodded twice.
And stared me in the eyes.

What she did to him was terrible.
There was no evidence of mental instability.
What was done to her was terrible.
There is no evidence of mental instability.

Millions of children starve, but not in England.
What we do not do for them is terrible.

Is England's love locked up in England?
There is no evidence of mental instability.

Only love can unlock locked-up love.

Unlock all of your love.
You have enough for this woman.
Unlock all of your love.
You have enough to feed all those millions of children.

Cry if you like.
Do something if you can. You can.

C

Ten Ways to Avoid Lending
Your Wheelbarrow to Anybody

After I'd been writing Great Poetry for about thirty-three years
I realised that I had accumulated a certain amount of capital on
Parnassus. So I went out and spent it all on a fine wooden wheel-
barrow. Then the trouble started. All sorts of tyro versifiers, son-
neteers and rhyme-mongers began to doggerel my footsteps, plead-
ing for the loan of my barrow. So I sat down and wrote...

1 PATRIOTIC

May I borrow your wheelbarrow?
— I didn't lay down my life in World War II
so that you could borrow my wheelbarrow.

2 SNOBBISH

May I borrow your wheelbarrow?
— Unfortunately David Bowie is using it.

3 OVERWEENING

May I borrow your wheelbarrow?
— It is too mighty a conveyance to be wielded
by any mortal save myself.

4 PIOUS

May I borrow your wheelbarrow?
— My wheelbarrow is reserved for religious ceremonies.

5 MELODRAMATIC

May I borrow your wheelbarrow?
— I would sooner be broken on its wheel
and buried in its barrow.

6 PATHETIC

May I borrow your wheelbarrow?
— I am dying of schizophrenia
and all you can talk about is wheelbarrows.

7 DEFENSIVE

May I borrow your wheelbarrow?
– Do you think I'm made of wheelbarrows?

8 SINISTER

May I borrow your wheelbarrow?
– It is full of blood.

9 LECHEROUS

May I borrow your wheelbarrow?
– Only if I can fuck your wife in it.

10 PHILOSOPHICAL

May I borrow your wheelbarrow?
– What is a wheelbarrow?

To a Russian Soldier in Prague

1968. TV and the newspapers were almost fanatically uninterested in my verses about Vietnam and the Bomb. But they certainly jumped at this one. No sooner had I recorded it for one of those mushroom TV youth shows than an *Evening Standard* reporter asked for it. Next day, there it was on the Londoner's Diary page together with an explanation that I was a left-wing poet. Those Tories who read it through to the end, however, were fairly disturbed by its equation of a new colonial power with an old one.

I've written far more of my political cartoon verses about the West than about the East. That's because I live in the West and sometimes know where I am in British and American culture. But I've made very few excursions to the East and, while I've been there, have seen very little and understood less.

I know that centralised great power Communism has no chance of working. It talks equality but creates Stalin. I know that Capitalism works very well for some people – the people of *The Tatler* – but is murderous for other people – the wretched of the earth. I do believe in a world in which food, wealth, land and power are shared equally. And I do believe in the old *Illuminatus!* motto: 'No communication is possible except between equals'. I could go on, but not in this book.

You are going to be hated by the people.

They will hate you over their freakish breakfast of tripe soup and
        pastries.
They will squint hatred at you on their way to pretend to work.
By the light of yellow beer they will hate you with jokes you'll
        never hear.

You're beginning to feel
Like a landlord in a slum
Like a white man in Harlem
Like a U.S. Marine in Saigon

Socialists are hated
By all who kill for profit and power.
But you are going to be hated by
The people – who are all different.
The people – who are all extraordinary.
The people – who are all of equal value.
Socialism is theirs, it was invented for them.
Socialism is theirs, it can only be made by them.

Africa, Asia and Latin America are screaming:
STARVATION. POVERTY. OPPRESSION.
When they turn to America.
They see only flames and children in the flames.
When they turn to England
They see an old lady in a golden wheelchair,
Share certificates in one hand, a pistol in the other.
When they turn to Russia
They see – you.

You are going to be hated
As the English have usually been hated.
The starving, the poor and the oppressed
Are turning, turning away.
While you nervously guard a heap of documents
They stagger away through the global crossfire
Towards revolution, towards socialism.

Vroomph! *or* The Popular Elastic Waist

This was one of my cut-up poems from the mid-sixties. Always wish I had time to do more of them. This was a cut-up of sentences from the *Sunday Times* Colour Magazine of 9th December 1967, which featured Civil Defence, Famous Footballers, The Girls of Thailand, Gangsters and several advertisements.

Juliet sighs. Romeo speaks.
Deep shelters are out of most people's reach.
The white tin is a simple gadget for pinpointing the size and position
of nuclear bursts.
Simply push the needle in, pump the handle, and
You haven't seen anything till you've seen the 200 pounds of beautiful
Louise
Tucked away in the secret, hardened, national seat of government,
Or balanced on bicycles while removing 12 shirts.
Yet, even when we made love, at a time when most
women are feeling romantic, she would start to
prattle away about
The Royal State Trumpeters of the Household Cavalry.

Stimulated by these breaks in the nuclear overcast,
the *Sunday Times* here offers what is probably the
first complete review of our Civil Defence
preparations,
A symbol of the virile, aggressive, muscular game which
one associates with a man who has twice broken the
same leg – and twice returned to the game.
This is the problem: whether to drink Cointreau neat
and slowly savour every warming sip,
Or hang from the tops of palm trees by our feet.

While we have the bomb it seems ridiculous not to be honest.
It works like this: the motor is powered by ordinary torch batteries.
The slightly wounded will be sent on their way, the severely wounded
left to
The Marquis de Ferrara.
Fill out the Panic Sheet.

Neither the *Sunday Times* nor its agents accepts any liability for loss or
The gruesome electric chair.
You see, we are unashamedly devoted to the kind
  of quiet courtesy
      which gets rarer
          every
              day.

Dumb Insolence

I started to practise dumb insolence at an early age. It can be a devastating piece of sabotage. When I was conscripted into the RAF I found that among the many charges they can lay on you there is one called *Dumb Insolence*. So I revised my tactic to *Disguised Dumb Insolence*.

I'm big for ten years old
Maybe that's why they get at me

Teachers, parents, cops
Always getting at me

When they get at me

I don't hit em
They can do you for that

I don't swear at em
They can do you for that

I stick my hands in my pockets
And stare at them

And while I stare at them
I think about sick

They call it dumb insolence

They don't like it
But they can't do you for it

Giving Potatoes

Long after this one became one of my most popular verses, especially with children, I wrote the following introductory verses:

> There was a Woman of the West
> A fisherman's lovely daughter
> She was so fair that many men
> Braved the wild seas to court her
>
> Some knelt before her with bouquets
> Of roses held aloft
> And some brought chocolate boxes
> With centres hard and soft
>
> Give your chocolates to the children
> Your bouquets to the bees
> For chocolates make me spotty
> And flowers make me sneeze
>
> It's only the potato
> Can warm my chilly blood
> Bring me the fine potato
> The incomparable spud
>
> From the refrigerating land of Finns
> From the Sudan's white heat
> They brought their best potatoes
> And they laid them at her feet...

The poem's fun to perform because you get to play all the different characters. My favourite is the Old Man.

STRONG MAN: Mashed potatoes cannot hurt you, darling
Mashed potatoes mean no harm
I have brought you mashed potatoes
From my mashed potato farm.

LADY: Take away your mashed potatoes
Leave them in the desert to dry
Take them away your mashed potatoes –
You look like shepherd's pie.

BRASH MAN: A packet of chips, a packet of chips,
Wrapped in the *Daily Mail*,
Golden and juicy and fried for a week
In the blubber of the Great White Whale.

LADY: Take away your fried potatoes
             Use them to clean your ears
             You can eat your fried potatoes
             With Birds-Eye frozen tears.

OLD MAN: I have borne this baked potato
             O'er the Generation Gap,
             Pray accept this baked potato
             Let me lay it in your heated lap.

LADY: Take away your baked potato
             In your fusty musty van
             Take away your baked potato
             You potato-skinned old man.

FRENCHMAN: She rejected all potatoes
             For a thousand nights and days
             Till a Frenchman wooed and won her
             With pommes de terre Lyonnaises.

LADY: Oh my corrugated lover
             So creamy and so brown
             Let us fly across to Lyons
             And lay our tubers down.

The Castaways *or* Vote for Caliban

This was inspired by Jules Verne's three-volume miracle *The Mysterious Island* in which a marooned group swiftly converts a desert island into a rough version of Paris, France.

It is written to be performed with a lot of gestures and jumping about, but it became a bit famous when it was set by the Northern Examining Association for its 'O' Level and CSE paper – without permission. At the front of several of my books I say that none of my poems should be used in connection with any exam whatsoever.

The Guardian had the bright idea of inviting me to sit the exam, so I did. Here are two of the questions:

> [A2] Study lines 15-37. Tom, Susan, Jim and Bill use their skills to help each other and Mary to live on the island. Which two of these people had the most necessary skills, in your opinion? Give reasons for your opinion. Why did you not choose the other two?

> [A3] Having studied lines 41-48, one reader says: 'The poet is not serious here. He is having a joke with us.' To what extent would you agree with the reader's opinion of lines 41-48? Give reasons.

I got full marks for the second question by writing: 'To no extent do I agree with the reader (the reader sounds a bit Japanese). The poem is a serious poem because poetry is serious because otherwise it would not be set for examinations because examinations are serious, in fact so serious that if I fail this exam I will probably never get a job and will be stuck on the end of a pier of lava for the rest of my natural, metaphorically speaking. The poem is about western civilisation, which is beyond a joke.'

However I fared far less well on most questions, in fact it might be hard to fare worse. I sat the exam at the same time as a group of 'O' Level students from Chetham's School in Manchester. The papers were marked blind by an independent examiner. I scored only fourteen marks out a possible forty and came next to bottom. The top scorer collected 35. She used phrases like 'civilised amenities'. She was called Lucy.

This teaches us to smile at watch-makers.

The Pacific Ocean –
A blue demi-globe.
Islands like punctuation marks.

A cruising airliner,
Passengers unwrapping pats of butter.
A hurricane arises,
Tosses the plane into the sea.

Five of them, flung on to an island beach,
Survived.
Tom the reporter.
Susan the botanist.
Jim the high-jump champion.
Bill the carpenter.
Mary the eccentric widow.

Tom the reporter sniffed out a stream of drinkable water.
Susan the botanist identified a banana tree.
Jim the high-jump champion jumped up and down and gave them
        each a bunch.
Bill the carpenter knocked up a table for their banana supper.
Mary the eccentric widow buried the banana skins,
But only after they had asked her twice.
They all gathered sticks and lit a fire.
There was an incredible sunset.

Next morning they held a committee meeting.
Tom, Susan, Jim and Bill
Voted to make the best of things.
Mary, the eccentric widow, abstained.

Tom the reporter killed several dozen wild pigs,
Tanned their skins into parchment
And printed the *Island News* with the ink of squids.

Susan the botanist developed new strains of banana
Which tasted of chocolate, beefsteak, peanut butter,
Chicken and bootpolish.

Jim the high-jump champion organised organised games
Which he always won easily.

Bill the carpenter constructed a wooden water wheel
And converted the water's energy into electricity.
Using iron ore from the hills, he constructed lampposts.

They all worried about Mary, the eccentric widow,
Her lack of confidence and her –
But there wasn't time to coddle her.

The volcano erupted, but they dug a trench
And diverted the lava into the sea
Where it formed a spectacular pier.
They were attacked by pirates but defeated them
With bamboo bazookas firing
Sea-urchins packed with home-made nitro-glycerine.
They gave the cannibals a dose of their own medicine
And survived an earthquake thanks to their skill in jumping.

Tom had been a court reporter
So he became the magistrate and solved disputes.
Susan the Botanist established
A university which also served as a museum.
Jim the high-jump champion
Was put in charge of law-enforcement –
Jumped on them when they were bad.
Bill the carpenter built himself a church,
Preached there every Sunday.

But Mary the eccentric widow...
Each evening she wandered down the island's main street,
Past the Stock Exchange, the Houses of Parliament,
The prison and the arsenal.
Past the Prospero Souvenir Shop,
Past the Robert Louis Stevenson Movie Studios,
Past the Daniel Defoe Motel
She nervously wandered and sat on the end of the pier of lava,

Breathing heavily,
As if at a loss,
As if at a lover,
She opened her eyes wide
To the usual incredible sunset.

My Parents

It was during my teens that I was shocked to discover that several of my friends disliked, despised or even hated their parents. I loved both of mine very much. I only remember writing one poem for my mother while she was alive and none for my father till after his death. Sorry.

I wrote this piece as my column for *Peace News*. Before I published it I sent it to my elder brother Jimmy, since I wouldn't have published it if he hadn't liked it. He did like it. Jimmy is two years older than me, Professor of Pharmacology at Bristol University and one day he'll make an amazing poem. But it's not written yet.

This is certainly prose, but I read it often at poetry readings because older people especially understand it so well. And because I enjoy thinking about my mother and father. I still value their opinions and feel their love shine on me.

My father died the other day and I would like to write about him. Because I think of them together, this means also writing about my mother, who died several years ago.

About a thousand people called her Kay, most of them people she helped at some time, for she was what chintzy villains call a "do-gooder". Nobody ever called her that to her face or in my family's hearing; if they had, she'd have felt sorry for them. Both her brothers were killed in the First World War. She wore two poppies on Remembrance Day. She divided her life between loving her family, bullying or laughing innumerable committees into action rather than talk, giving, plotting happiness for other people, and keeping up an exuberant correspondence with several hundred friends.

She was not afraid of anyone. She was right. A Fabian near-pacifist, she encouraged me to argue, assuming right-wing positions sometimes so that I was forced to fight and win the discussion.

She tried to hoist the whole world on her shoulders. After each of her first two cancer operations, on her breasts, she seemed to clench her fists and double the energy with which she gave. She wasn't interested in unshared pleasure.

After the second operation she answered the door one day to a poor woman whom she didn't know. The woman asked where 'the wise woman' lived. My mother knew who she meant – a rich clairvoyant who lived down the road. Not trusting that particular witch, my mother asked what was wrong. The poor woman's doctor had told her she must have a breast removed, and she was very scared. My mother said, but there's nothing to that, look – and she took out the two rolled socks which she kept in her empty brassière and threw them up into the sunlight and then caught them again. So the poor woman came in, drank tea, forgot many fears, and went away knowing that she had seen the wise woman.

People called my father Jock. Face tanned from working in his garden, he survived four years in the trenches of the First World War. He spoke very little. When he talked it was either very funny or very important. He only spoke to me about his war twice, and then briefly. In my teens I wrote a short, Owen-influenced poem about the war. My father read it, then told me of a friend who, during the lull between bombardments, fell to all fours, howled like an animal and was never cured.

Usually he avoided company. There was something in other people which frightened him. He was right. At the seaside he would sit on the farthest-out rock and fish peacefully. When visitors called at our house he would generally disappear into his jungle of raspberry canes and lurk.

Maybe there were twenty or thirty people in then world whose company he really enjoyed. They were lucky; he was a lovely man. Like Edward Lear, he was most at ease with children, who instantly read, in the lines radiating from corners of his eyes, that this was a man who understood their games and jokes.

He was short and lean and had fantastic sprouting Scottish eyebrows. He was a research chemist, but that didn't mean he only took an interest and pride in my elder brother's scientific work. He let me see how glad he was that I wrote and I still remember the stories he used to write for me and my brother.

A year or so before he died he was in London for the day. My father sometimes voted Tory, sometimes Liberal, but when he began to talk about Vietnam that day, his face became first red and then white with anger about the cruelty and stupidity of the war. I seldom saw him angry and never so angry as at that moment, a man of seventy, not much interested in politics, all the grief of 1914-18 marching back into his mind.

People sometimes talk as if the ideological conflicts between generations have to be fought out bloodily, as if it is inevitable that children should grow to hate their parents. I don't believe this. Our family was lucky: my brother and I were always free to choose for ourselves – knowing that, however odd our decisions, we were trusted and loved. We all loved one another and this love was never shadowed.

Apeman Give a Poetry Reading
and
The Apeman's Hairy Body Song

As one of the elder statesmen of Boogieville, I do like to encourage young talent, however raw. One of the junior poets I have nurtured over the years has been Apeman Mudgeon, whom I discovered in the Jungle of Eden, under a hot-dog stand.

I have often allocated him a "spot" in my poetry programmes, albeit that he has sometimes abused that privilege. Well, youth will have its fling – but let Apeman Mudgeon speak for himself:

Hello folk! Apeman Mudgeon. Mr Mitchell say I print two poems in book. Two poems. Big deal, Mr Mitchell. Mr Mitchell got 38 poems in book. Count 'em. 38. Huh. But Apeman poems fine poems everyone love the Apeman. Kids in Belfast made up tune for Apeman's Hairy Body Song. Apeman sing it for you now. Don't worry bout Mr Mitchell saying 'No time now' – Everybody sing along with Apeman!

Apeman Give a Poetry Reading

Apeman travel much in jungle
Sometimes he swing for many miles
To taxi down in some new clearing.
No concert posters up on trees.
Tiger who arranged the gig
Has gone down with sabre-toothache.
Gazelle apologises nervously.
Apeman and gazelle shift rocks around
To form a semi-circle.
Two or three crocodiles trundle in.
Four flying squirrels. One sloth.
Various reptiles and a fruit-bat.
Suddenly – ten-eleven multi-colour birds.
Apeman cheers up.
Gazelle checks time by the sun,

Introduces apeman.
Apeman performs a series
Of variegated apeman howls –
Comic howls, sad howls, angry-desperate howls.
Apeman runs out of howl, sits down.
Senior crocodile asks question:
What use is howling?
Howling does not change jungle.
Apeman stares at him,
Nods, shakes his head, gives up.
Animals begin to drift to holes and nests.
Apeman swings home heavily through the gloom.
If you meet apeman in this mood
Give him a hug.
Unless your name is Boa-constrictor.

The Apeman's Hairy Body Song

Happy to be hairy
Happy to be hairy
When the breezes tickle
The hairs of my body

Happy to be hairy
Happy to be hairy
Next best thing
To having feathers

On the Beach at Cambridge

A TV documentary. A bureaucrat was being interviewed about his work: 'Well, I'm in charge of files on personnel. I keep the files up to date.' Interviewer: 'And what happens to your job in case of a nuclear alert?' Bureaucrat: ' I have an entirely similar set of files in a Government office in an underground bunker. I go down there and continue to maintain my files.' Interviewer: 'You're married, aren't you?' Bureaucrat: 'Yes, we've got two children, boy and a girl.' Interviewer: 'And what happens to your wife and children in case –' Bureaucrat: '– Yes, well unfortunately there isn't room for them in the bunker. But we talked it over. We agreed somebody had to carry on...'

Listening to him, I felt there was something lacking. I couldn't give him an imagination, or a soul. But I could try to give him a poem.

At the time, early 1981, I was living in Cambridge on a Judith E. Wilson Fellowship, normally awarded to the least academic writer in the known universe. An anti-bomb demo was coming up at the local bunker in Brooklands Avenue. So that's where I set the poem.

I began writing with some bitterness towards the bureaucrat. By the time I finished rewriting the sixth draft, I felt some love for him. So the poem helped me, anyway.

I am assistant to the Regional Commissioner
At Block E, Brooklands Avenue,
Communications Centre for Region 4,
Which used to be East Anglia.

I published several poems as a young man
But later found I could not meet my own high standards
So tore up all my poems and stopped writing.
(I stopped painting at eight and singing at five.)
I was seconded to Block E
From the Ministry for the Environment.

Since there are no established poets available
I have come out here in my MPC
(Maximum Protective Clothing),
To dictate some sort of poem or word-picture
Into a miniature cassette recorder.

When I first stepped out of Block E on to this beach
I could not record any words at all,
So I chewed two of the orange-flavoured pills
They give us for morale, switched on my Sony
And recorded this:

I am standing on the beach at Cambridge.
I can see a group in their MPC
Pushing Hoover-like and Ewbank-like machines
Through masses of black ashes.
The taller men are soldiers or police,
The others, scientific supervisors.
This group moves slowly across what seems
Like an endless car park with no cars at all.

I think that, in one moment,
All the books in Cambridge
Leapt off their shelves,
Spread their wings
And became white flames
And then black ash.
And I am standing on the beach at Cambridge.

You're a poet, said the Regional Commissioner,
Go out and describe that lot.

The University Library – a little hill of brick-dust.
King's College Chapel – a dune of stone-dust.
The sea is coming closer and closer.

The clouds are edged with green,
Sagging low under some terrible weight.
They move more rapidly than usual.

Some younger women with important jobs
Were admitted to Block E

But my wife was a teacher in her forties.
We talked it over
When the nature of the crisis became apparent.
We agreed somebody had to carry on.
That day I kissed her goodbye as I did every day
At the door of our house in Chesterton Road.
I kissed my son and my daughter goodbye.
I drove to Block E beside Hobson's Brook.
I felt like a piece of paper
Being torn in half.

And I am standing on the beach at Cambridge.
Some of the men in their MPC
Are sitting on the ground in the black ashes.
One is holding his head in both his hands.

I was forty-two three weeks ago.
My children painted me
Bright-coloured cards with poems for my birthday.
I stuck them with Blu-Tack on the kitchen door.
I can remember the colours.

But in one moment all the children in Cambridge
Spread their wings
And became white flames
And then black ash.

And the children of America, I suppose.
And the children of Russia, I suppose.

And I am standing on the beach at Cambridge
And I am watching the broad black ocean tide
Bearing on its shoulders its burden of black ashes.

And I am listening to the last words of the sea
As it beats its head against the dying land.

[Cambridge, March 1981]

Beattie Is Three

This is probably my best poem, certainly the one most people like. It's especially popular in prisons.

Beattie is my youngest daughter and she's always had a very strong personality, to put it nicely. And like many kids of three years old, she had begun to think of herself as almost a grown-up, perfectly capable of walking downstairs by herself.

We were living in Lower Hardacre, a beautiful old stone farmhouse in the Yorkshire Dales. The stairs had a rough cord carpet. As we were about half-way down I realised that I was intensely happy. I recorded that happiness as soon as I could.

Many years later Beattie was a rebel teenager and our domestic wars were frequent and terrible. But she came along anyway one day when I launched one of my books by reading two poems from the counter of Bernard Stone's beautiful bookshop. The second poem was *Beattie Is Three*. As I said: 'I ask for her hand.' I suddenly felt a hand take mine, looked down and saw Beattie holding on and smiling. So the poem, despite all our battles, had acted as a kind of promise between us, a keepsake, a rose, a blessing.

Younger children often ask me which of my poems I like best and I recite them this one. Most of them seem to have younger brothers and sisters, so they can understand it, even though I have to explain what consolation is.

At the top of the stairs
I ask for her hand. O.K.
She gives it to me.
How her fist fits my palm,
A bunch of consolation.
We take our time
Down the steep carpetway
As I wish silently
That the stairs were endless.

A Tourist Guide to England

This was written for a poetry conference in Lahti, Finland. I wanted to satirise the country in which I've lived all my life, despite being, legally, Scots and therefore an alien being. But, since there were writers from greater powers, like the USA and USSR at the conference, I wanted to end it in such a way that they would consider their own countries' crimes, whether in Vietnam or Czechoslovakia or at home. So I twisted its tail into some kind of corkscrew.

£ Welcome to England!
England is a happy country.

£ Here is a happy English businessman.
Hating his money, he spends it all
On bibles for Cambodia
And a charity to preserve
The Indian Cobra from extinction.

£ I'm sorry you can't see our happy coalminers.
Listen hard and you can hear them
Singing Welsh hymns far underground.
Oh. The singing seems to have stopped.

£ No, that is not Saint Francis of Assisi.
That is a happy English policeman.

£ Here is a happy black man.
No, it is not illegal to be black. Not yet.

£ Here are the slums.
They are preserved as a tourist attraction.
Here is a happy slum-dweller.
Hello, slum-dweller!
No, his answer is impossible to translate.

£ Here are some happy English schoolchildren.
See John. See Susan. See Mike.
They are studying for their examinations.
Study, children, study!
John will get his 'O' Levels
And an 'O' Level job and an 'O' Level house and an 'O' Level wife.
Susan will get her 'A' Levels
And an 'A' Level job and an 'A' Level house and an 'A' Level husband.
Mike will fail.

£ Here are some happy English soldiers.
They are going to make the Irish happy.

£ No, please understand.
We understand the Irish
Because we've been sending soldiers to Ireland
For hundreds and hundreds of years.

£ First we tried to educate them
With religion, famine and swords.
But the Irish were slow to learn.

£ Then we tried to educate them
With reason, poverty and unemployment.
They became silent, sullen, violent.

£ So now we are trying to educate them
With truncheons, gas, rubber bullets,
Steel bullets, internment and torture.
We are trying to teach the Irish,
To be as happy as us.

£ So please understand us
And if your country
Should be forced to educate
Another country in the same way,
Or your own citizens in the same way –
We will try to understand you.

Victor Jara of Chile

1973. After the fascist coup in Chile. Alvaro Bunster, Allende's ambassador in London, asked Celia and I if we could house three Chilean refugees. (Those with British passports were being allowed in.) They arrived, Joan Jara the dancer and her two young daughters, Mandy and Manuela. Joan was married to Victor Jara, who had been murdered in the first two days of the coup. We talked about what was happening in Chile, about how Victor died and then we talked, at length, about how Victor lived. Every night Joan was at meetings all over Britain telling Victor's story and the story of Chile. It was vital to find other ways of doing this.

The BBC at this time decided to run a "topical drama" slot, so we offered the idea of a play about Victor's life. They commissioned it, I wrote two drafts. The play was publicly announced and, even before it was written, was attacked in the press as being predictably left-wing, given the subject and my track record. The BBC accepted my play, but, in the same phone call, postponed it indefinitely. Two months had gone by since Victor's death and they thought it was no longer topical.

Eventually a fine film was made of Joan's testimony. She and her daughters have now returned to Chile. Using the royalties from Victor's records, Joan has founded a dance company called Espiral which works with all sorts of people in and around Santiago, especially the poor and the children of the poor. As I write, Chile is still not a safe place for Joan, Mandy or Manuela, but Chile is their home.

I wrote this ballad to the tune of Woody Guthrie's *Dear Mrs Roosevelt*. Joan approved the poem, which I sent to Arlo Guthrie, hoping he'd sing it. He set it to a new tune of his own and recorded it.

I've performed it at every reading for adults I've done since 1973. But reciting it in Chile in 1989 was different. It was read first in Spanish by Mauricio Redoles, the Chilean poet, at song, dance and poetry rallies. When the ballad mentioned Allende, the audience broke into cheers and chants. When the generals were mentioned, the air was painful with whistles. At the end, audiences chanted their tribute to Victor Jara — singer, songwriter, guitarist and comrade.

Victor Jara of Chile
Lived like a shooting star
He fought for the people of Chile
With his songs and his guitar

And his hands were gentle
His hands were strong

Victor Jara was a peasant
Worked from a few years old
He sat upon his father's plough
And watched the earth unfold

And his hands were gentle
His hands were strong

When the neighbours had a wedding
Or one of their children died
His mother sang all night for them
With Victor by her side

And his hands were gentle
His hands were strong

He grew to be a fighter
Against the people's wrongs
He listened to their grief and joy
And turned them into songs

And his hands were gentle
His hands were strong

He sang about the copper miners
And those who work the land
He sang about the factory workers
And they knew he was their man

And his hands were gentle
His hands were strong

He campaigned for Allende
Working night and day
He sang: take hold of your brother's hand
The future begins today

And his hands were gentle
His hands were strong

The bloody generals seized Chile
They arrested Victor then
They caged him in a stadium
With five thousand frightened men

And his hands were gentle
His hands were strong

Victor stood in the stadium
His voice was brave and strong
He sang for his fellow-prisoners
Till the guards cut short his song

And his hands were gentle
His hands were strong

They broke the bones in both his hands
They beat his lovely head
They tore him with electric shocks
After two long days of torture they shot him dead

And his hands were gentle
His hands were strong

And now the Generals rule Chile
And the British have their thanks
For they rule with Hawker Hunters
And they rule with Chieftain tanks

And his hands were gentle
His hands were strong

Victor Jara of Chile
Lived like a shooting star
He fought for the people of Chile
With his songs and his guitar

And his hands were gentle
His hands were strong

Sorry Bout That

I don't know who coined the motto *Never apologise, never explain*,
but I bet it was somebody with a salary and a pension. I spend
several hours a day apologising, no, sorry, I exaggerate, at least
an hour a day. I had to give up tennis early because I said sorry
whenever I won a point and sorry whenever I lost one. Finally I
thought I ought to wrap all my apologies up into one rubber ball
of sorry which I could bounce around at the end of each poetry
performance in order to say sorry for all the shortcomings of the
evening. Before you read it, I should warn you that the first line
is an example of the kind of pretentious generalisation which gives
poetry such a bad name. Not that I'm claiming to write poetry...

Truth is a diamond
A diamond is hard
You don't exist
Without a Barclaycard

Sorry bout that
Sorry bout that
Even South African cops
Do the sorry bout that

They showed me the world and said:
What do you think?
I said: half about women
And half about drink

And I'm sorry bout that
Sorry bout that
Mother, I need that booze
And I'm sorry bout that

If you cut your conscience
Into Kennomeat chunks
You can get elected
To the House of Drunks

Sorry bout that
Sorry bout that
You'll never have to think again
And I'm sorry bout that

You can do the Skull
Or the Diplomat
But I do a dance called
The Sorry Bout That

Do the Mighty Whitey
Or the Landlord Rat
But I'll keeping grooving to
The Sorry Bout That

Sorry bout that
Sorry bout that
They make me dance with pistols and ten to one
I'm sorry bout that

I saw Money walking
Down the road
Claws like an eagle
And a face like a toad

Well I know your name baby
Seen you before
Slapping on your make-up
For the Third World War

Sorry bout that
Sorry bout that
Someone set the world on fire
And I'm sorry bout that

Goodbye

And that's all except –

Goodbye

He breathed in air, he breathed out light –
Charlie Parker was my delight.

Adrian Mitchell was born in London in 1932. He worked as a reporter on the *Oxford Mail* and the *Evening Standard* from 1955 to 1963, and subsequently as a freelance journalist for the *Daily Mail, Sun, Sunday Times, New Statesman*, etc, before quitting journalism for full-time writing in 1966.

POETRY: He was one of the leaders of the revival in oral poetry in Britain which started in 1959, and has given more than a thousand performances of his poetry – in clubs, pubs, theatres, colleges, schools, prisons, concert halls, village halls and parks all over Britain as well as in Austria, Canada, Israel, Cuba, the USA, Australia, Finland, Switzerland, Bulgaria, Belgium, Holland, the USSR, Italy, Germany, Spain, Chile and Jugoslavia. He was guest poet on Paul McCartney's 1991 World Tour (Southend leg).

His books of poetry include *Out Loud, The Apeman Cometh, For Beauty Douglas: Collected Poems 1953-79* (Allison & Busby, 1982), *On the Beach at Cambridge* (Allison & Busby, 1984), *Love Songs of World War Three* (Allison & Busby/W.H. Allen, 1989), *Greatest Hits: His 40 Golden Greats* (Bloodaxe Books, 1991) and, for children, *Nothingmas Day* and *All My Own Stuff*. He is also the editor of the children's anthology *Strawberry Drums*.

PLAYWRIGHT: His plays, all of them with songs, include *Tyger* (National Theatre), *Man Friday* (7:84), *Mind Your Head* (Liverpool Everyman), *A Seventh Man* (Foco Novo), *White Suit Blues* (Nottingham Playhouse), *Uppendown Mooney* (Welfare State International), *The White Deer* (Unicorn Theatre for Children), *Hoagy, Bix and Wolfgang Beethoven Bunkhaus* (King's Head Theatre), *In the Unlikely Event of an Emergency* (South West Music Theatre), *Mowgli's Jungle* (Contact Theatre, Manchester), *A Child's Christmas in Wales* (with Jeremy Brooks, Great Lakes Festival), *The Wild Animal Song Contest* (Unicorn Theatre for Children), *Animal Farm* (lyrics, National Theatre), *C'mon Everybody* (Tricycle Theatre), *Satie Day/Night* (Lyric Hammersmith), *The Pied Piper* (National Theatre), *The Snow Queen* (ESIPA at the Egg, Albany, USA) and *Anna on Anna* (Offstage Downstairs).

STAGE ADAPTATIONS: He has adapted many foreign plays for the stage, including Peter Weiss' *Marat/Sade* (Royal Shakespeare Company), José Triana's *The Criminals* (Royal Shakespeare Company), Calderón's *Life's a Dream* (with John Barton, Royal Shakespeare Company), Ibsen's *Peer Gynt* (Oxford Playhouse), Calderón's *The Mayor of Zalamea* (National Theatre), Gogol's *The Government Inspector* (National Theatre), Calderón's *The Great Theatre of the World*

(Mediaeval Players) and Lope de Vega's *Fuente Ovejuna* (National Theatre).

FILMS & TV PLAYS: Television plays include *Daft as a Brush, Silver Giant, Wooden Dwarf, The Fine Art of Bubble Blowing, Something Down There Is Crying, Glad Day* and *You Must Believe All This*.
Films include *Man Friday, The Body* (commentary) and *The Tragedy of King Real*.

FICTION: His novels include *If You See Me Comin', The Bodyguard* and *Wartime*. He has written many stories for children, including the *Our Mammoth* and *The Baron* series for Walker Books.

FELLOWSHIPS ETC: He was Granada Fellow in the Arts at Lancaster University, 1968-70; Fellow at Wesleyan University, 1972; Resident Writer at the Sherman Theatre in Cardiff, 1974-75; Visiting Writer at Billericay Comprehensive School, 1977-79; Judith E. Wilson Fellow at Cambridge University, 1980-81; and Resident Writer at the Unicorn Theatre for Children, 1982-83. He has also been awarded the Gold Medal of the Theatre of Poetry, Varna, Bulgaria, and is a Fellow of the Royal Society of Literature.